MULTILINGUAL
— Your Way to —
SUCCESS
Fall in Love with Your Passion

MULTILINGUAL
— *Your Way to* —
SUCCESS
Fall in Love with Your Passion

Authored by
ANITA PUROHIT

Penman Books

Office No. 303, Kumar House Building,
D Block, Central Market, Opp PVR Cinema,
Prashant Vihar, Delhi 110085, India
Website: www.penmanbooks.com
Email: publish@penmanbooks.com

First Published by Penman Books 2019
Copyright © Monika Singh | Kailash Pinjani 2019
All Rights Reserved.

Title: Multilingual Your Way to Success
ISBN: 978-93-89024-04-3

Dedicated to...

I dedicate this book to
my loving parents,
without whom this wouldn't
have been possible.

Preface

"The power of being a linguist is indisputable.
The power of multilingual skills
is transformational."

Languages have the power to inspire, influence and motivate people. So why do so many great people fail to deliver on this promise?

In my understanding, often the problem is not to do with the language itself but the way we think about, and use that language.

My journey into the world of languages started when I taught as a Professor of Physics in Mumbai University. During that time in 1991, I got interested in languages and started learning

Italian at the University's Department of Foreign Languages.

Later, in 2001, I started learning Mandarin with a Taiwanese trainer by the name of Yang Yulan. My curiosity to learn different languages did not end there. In 2013, I started learning Thai from a native teacher. Gradually, my interest deepened as I not only learnt the syntax, the grammar and the vocabulary but through the foreign language, also the culture, habits, the philosophy, value system and the way of life of a community. In this search, I was fascinated with the discovery that the Chinese language, Mandarin is the world's most spoken/ written language. Over time, through Mandarin, I started access to the literature on Taoism and learnt about the life-transforming teachings of the Chinese philosopher Confucius. Through this journey, I figured out that the exercise of learning a foreign language is incomplete, if the learner does not simultaneously attempt to learn more about the religion, food habits, dress sense and the culture of the people who speak that language. Since I have myself gained so much from my passion for foreign languages that finally with the encouragement of my students and well-wishers, I had this opportunity to put my thoughts and experiences into this book.

Inside this book, you'll learn how to implement your own experiences, emotions and vulnerabilities to build a connection with your audience through the use of various languages and take them on a journey that can ultimately lead to action.

Additionally, in this book, you will discover the key to:

- Motivate & inspire others through the use of various languages.

- Authentically connect with audience.

- Transcend other ways of thinking.

- Make your communication more influential.

I hope that you enjoy this book as much as I enjoyed putting it together for you.

Anita Purohit

Foreword

It is a matter of immense pleasure that one of our alumni, Ms. Anita Purohit has authored a book – *Multilingual Your Way to Success*.

Learning more than your mother tongue and Forging ahead into a matching multilingual environment, throws open to the generations, myriads of opportunities, where the students can choose an area of their choice and inclination.

I have known Anita since the time she first came to our institute to learn basic Chinese. Right from the word 'go' she exhibited sharp keenness, unflinching focus and warm enthusiasm to learn Chinese language. Despite her multifarious commitments, right from managing her own Training Academy, to taking care of her home, she has always shown extraordinary devotion to language learning.

That has been the key to her systematic progress in the Chinese class and reaching where she has reached now, her sedulous efforts and courage to write this book are admirable. I wish her all the success and hope that the readers will feel purposefully benefitted by what the book has to offer.

Col N S Rawat
Former Executive Director
India China Chamber of Commerce & Industry

About the Author

*"A Candle Burns itself to illumine others
surrounding it."*

Anita is a best-selling author, a successful, certified trainer, a unique educator and counselor who reaches out to over 1000 people, across the world, every year.

She commands a rich and diverse experience of over 25 years in various areas of counseling and guiding students from different disciplines.

A life-long devotee of Lord Krishna, she is presently the Director of Purohit Academy at Mumbai.

A firm believer in 'Quality over Quantity,' Anita's mission is to touch and take people's lives on an altogether different level, through value-based education.

Acheivements

Originally from Orissa, this unassuming educator migrated to Mumbai and started teaching at Vidyanagari, Kalina University, Mumbai. Anita's thirst for knowledge inspired her to learn Italian and soon she developed an insatiable appetite for other foreign languages, as well. Currently, she is well-versed in Italian; understands French and Spanish; speaks Chinese and Thai, also knows Oriya, English and Hindi.

> *When former model, Madhu Sapre got married in November 2001 to an Italian, she asked for Anita's services as her interpreter!*

As an Italian language trainer, translator, and interpreter in the metro city of Mumbai, Anita has travelled far and wide. She holds a diploma in Italian language from Delhi Italian consulate.

> *Anita was the interpreter when the owner of Little Italia restaurant wanted to converse with his Italian-born chef, who did not know English!*

As the promoter of Purohit Academy, she has always striven to offer high quality educational services in foreign languages. With a work experience of over two decades and a half, she has trained over (1500) senior executives in the past two years.

She has an unbeatable record of language training & counseling. Four students whose study visa was summarily rejected, until she appeared on the scene and with her help, they finally reached their dream destination and have now carved out a strong niche for themselves in their respective careers.

Contents

CHAPTER
One

Languages – Opening Up A World of Possibilities

*"One language sets you in a corridor for life.
Two languages open every door along the way."*

—Frank Smith

How far does this quote stand true in your life? In the present scenario, where we have begun to see the entire world as a 'family' it surely does.

Each day, we watch world leaders interacting and discussing issues of mutual interest that impact their countries on the global platform with the help of an expert translator, but just imagine the impact, were they able to directly converse in each other's language? Undoubtedly, the conversation would be far more relaxed, open, emotionally-intelligent and productive.

Heard this wisecrack? "To have another language is to possess a second soul" said Charlemagne. Being bilingual could be a way to see the world in two different ways or perspectives. Because, very often, having the rare ability to speak in two languages can feel like having two separate identities. It gives the ability to see the world through other's eyes.

Small wonder, talking to another person in his/her language helps you to relate to him/her better. America has around 41 deaf sign languages. Spain, Italy and France are the birthplaces of some of these sign languages. Just consider we are talking about a person who can neither hear, nor speak. Yet they have different sign languages based on the birthplace of that language. Then why shouldn't people blessed with the power of speech try bilingualism, if not multilingualism?

Learning a new language is a major plus in anyone's life. The world can then be your oyster. Communicating and speaking in one language is a basic human need. But being conversant in more than one spoken language definitely opens up the doors of several possibilities.

In any country, as a child grows up, he/she leans to grasp the language(s) of the culture(s) he/she is born into. But as he/she grows older they begin exploring the world around them. Now they have access to more opportunities; more choices. Being multilingual means your voice has better chances of being heard, outside of your birth country.

Fact File

- An estimated 7,000 different languages are spoken around the world.

- More 50% of these world languages have no written form.

- World's most extensively spoken languages are: Mandarin Chinese, English, Spanish, Hindi, Arabic, Bengali, Russian, Portuguese, Japanese, German and French.

- Approximately 75% of the world's population does not speak English.

- United Nation's official languages in use are: English, French, Spanish, Chinese, Russian and Arabic.

You may want to know why multilingualism is important in the era of Google Translate. Can the knowledge of an additional language get me the next raise?

Can it make me happier than I am?

My simple and straight-forward answer to these questions is - Yes, it can and it does!

You may not believe me, but leaning a new language is the secret formula for raising smart children.

It will awaken you to all the rich possibilities available in that country.

Do You Know Why German Language Is So Popular With Indian Students?

Do you know how many students enroll for German language classes every year?

Literally thousands! Guess why? Because, Germany is perhaps the only western country, where there is no tuition fee for post graduate studies even for foreign students. Their one requirement is that the foreign student should know German. On average, it takes just one year for an Indian student to master German language and tap into the opportunity. And most smart Indian students, who want to further their career abroad, they do get there.

The result is that, the number of Indian students in Germany has grown by 13.14% over the last year and stands at 17,570 (Winter Semester 2017-18), according to the latest data released by the Federal Statistical Office of Germany.

You can easily outreach to the people and places which are otherwise out of bound, just by learning their language. Imagine the fun of making friends on a train in China through Mandarin or discussing politics in Arabic with an Egyptian, or even learn about the marvels of the deaf culture through ASL (American Sign Language) and maybe translate between Hungarian and Portuguese at a social gathering and make your audience go dumbstruck with awe! Experience sounds amazing! And learning feels a bit daunting! But, believe me; it's doable with very little effort. This book will explain how.

Don't Be a Frog in the Well; Go For a Change of Perspective

A team of psychologists led by Prof. Keysar, of the University of Chicago conducted a chain of experiments in April last year. Their objective was to determine what effect thinking in a foreign language has on the final decision- making. The subjects were executives from U.S and Korea. The sample size was 300.

"It was found that thinking in a second language reduced deep-seated, misleading biases that unduly influence how risks and benefits are perceived," reported the Wired Newspaper. In simple language, what it implies is that thinking in a foreign language makes decisions-making more rational; more meaningful, or rather more intelligent.

Undoubtedly, language has the strength and ability to bring about a radical change in our perceived notions. A modified and improved outlook towards the world can create infinite possibilities. The outcome? Globalization in a true sense.

What is the Real Purpose of Language Learning?

Simply put, language is an instrument to communicate your feelings. It is not just a string of words. It is a basis on which you build and share ideas, thoughts, objectives and beliefs. Your language also speaks a great deal about your personality. While you learn 'what' you speak, you also learn 'how' you speak, in terms of tone and tonality. Language is also a cultural tool that binds people. Whenever you move out of the comfort zone of your culture, the familiarity breaks down. You will not be able hold a conversation and your speech will create confusion. Sometimes the language barrier can give wrong signals, because language is an 'expression' of who or what you are.

As a beginner, it does not matter as to how evolved you are in the use of a particular language. On the contrary, growing laterally in one language can after a while, limit your perception and you do not end up gaining much. Mastering just one language is like you have one color to paint your picture of life.

Knowing other languages will add different shades and depth to that picture. Let us imagine you are in a foreign language learning program, where you learnt Chinese grammar for beginners. Soon, you got fluent in it. And before you know, you are reading their wonderful literature, their scriptures and absorbing all the color shades of their ancient cultural development. I bet, you can begin to feel drawn into a different reality altogether. I know it because I have inhabited that space and am thoroughly enjoying my stay there.

> ## Get Your Second Intellect
>
> - Speaking a second language can subconsciously change us.
>
> - Learning a new language will give you an authentic view of that new culture, belief and thinking.
>
> - Creating an emotional awareness about the other people's feelings in your heart and mind.
>
> - Leading to completely new way to look at things.

Trust me, and I speak from many years of experience, if your C.V lists more than the mother tongue as your linguistic accomplishment, it will set you apart. You will be heavily rated as an employee for the global business world. In scientific language, "Bilingualism is known give a cognitive boost," which means that its value-adds to your intellect.

How Do Language Dynamics Work?

1. **Geographically** – Arms you with a linguistic skill to travel effectively

2. **Economically** – Preparedness to be a part of a new cultural experience

3. **Communication** – Gives you the expertise to hold a meaningful dialogue

4. **Knowledge and Media** – Means to absorb their news media

5. **Diplomacy** – Finesse to handle international ties

As the world grows closer, there is a surge in the need to engage. Learning diverse languages is a must. In the multipolar world, knowing only English will not suffice. Many international corporates today run their zonal offices outside English-speaking countries. Also, the U.S based corporations are now aware that to spread their wings, they should say, 'How are you?' with a global reach and impact, delivered, ideally in the local dialect.

A Trick to Learn a New Language Faster

A detailed analysis done on language learning showed that:

"Studying the first 1000 most frequently used words in the language will familiarize you with 76.0% of all vocabulary in non-fiction literature, 79.6% of all vocabulary in fiction literature, and 87.8% of vocabulary in oral speech.

Studying the 2000 most frequently used words will familiarize you with 84% of vocabulary in non-fiction, 86.1% of vocabulary in fictional literature, and 92.7% of vocabulary in oral speech.

And studying the 3000 most frequently used words will familiarize you with 88.2% of vocabulary in non-fiction, 89.6% of vocabulary in fiction, and 94.0% of vocabulary in oral speech."

Flummoxed?

Let's simplify.

On an average if you can muster 1000 words of a language it will signify the best use of your time, since learning an extra 1000 words will only escalate your oral speech capacity to five percent more. (88% to 93%).

The long and short of our discussion is that leaning a new language will throw open a window to the human community's soul. Creating a world with shared perspective can pave way for genuine empathy, happiness and progress.

CHAPTER *Two*

Multilingualism… What it Means?

"If we spoke a different language,
we would perceive a somewhat different world."

—Ludwig Wittgenstein

Wittgenstein was an Austrian philosopher. Today after almost 100 years, his words still ring true. The good, old man must be smiling up there.

Psychological studies have found that more than 50% of the world's population is bilingual. An approximately 3.5 billion people use more than one language to converse on a day to day basis. Multilingualism is a natural phenomenon lying dormant in every human being. It is not something off beat or rare. "Given the appropriate environment, two languages are as normal as two lungs" said one expert. (Cook 2002:23).

The exact definition of multilingualism is at a debatable ground however. A kind of linguistic continuum has been formed with two schools of thoughts. One extreme says multilingualism is complete knowledge and command over the other language. The expected expertise is to the level of a homegrown native. The other extreme believes, multilingualism means speaking the other language at the tourist level. Describing it as minimum words, phrases and sentences that a tourist would learn to manage a foreign trip using one new language.

Fact File

- A Being bi/multilingual is not normal.
- To be bi-/multilingual, you need to be highly skilled in both/all languages like the locals.
- Childhood bilingualism could be damaging to linguistic and cognitive progress resulting in lower grades at school.
- Our time-starved, over-burdened children do not have sufficient time to learn two languages.
- Why puzzle children with two languages?
- Bi/multilingual people have lesser vocabulary volume and are not stronger in 'verbal fluency chores' than the monolingual people.

Since 1992, Vivian Cook, a linguist has been maintaining that, most multilingual speakers fall in between these two extreme meanings. He came up with the term *'multi-competent'*.

Multilingualism, according to Cook comes with various psychological, social and lifestyle benefits. Researchers have presented a long list of health advantages springing from speaking more than one language. Believe it or not, faster recovery from a stroke and postponement in the occurrence of dementia are just a few of them.

Advantage Multilingualism

It is good for your brain – It alters your brain's framework and enhances its functioning in several scientific ways. Along with an improved memory it will help in better information-processing and easy multi-tasking.

Your travel companion – An overseas trip means you will be dependent on a tour guide for your travel experience. In the bargain, you might miss out a less explored location which could be dream come true for you. But it may not be one of the popular places on to do list of the guide. On the contrary, if you could speak the local language you could discover several new places on your own.

Multiply your hiring prospects- Most of the businesses today function in a workplace full of diversity, with reference to the workforce and client base. International corporate houses would definitely prefer multilingual or bilingual employees since they have a global spread. For professionals such as teachers and social workers, being multilingual would be a huge turn around if they are in a new country.

Pushing the boundaries of educational horizons- Many programs and courses abroad call for specific language requirements. Also knowing a second language creates an instant positive impression while applying for Ph.Ds. graduate schools and so on. Bilingualism will offer you a chance to use the new source material such as content from foreign language speakers, literature and researches that are not published in English.

Have You Heard This?

"Lost in translation" is not a myth. The simplest example is the sub titles on a film. Have you noticed? Sometimes the words in your native language loose meaning when written as English subtitles. This happens because some words, concepts, notions and ideas cannot be expressed with equal ease in another language.

For instance, English would not be able to match the levels of respect addressed and used in Korean or Japanese.

Whether you grow up as a bilingual or become one as an adult, you will have lots to gain by picking up oral dexterity in another language. The human race is naturally synced and programmed to sense, pick up and learn languages. Though you may not be bilingual today, as a kid everyone goes through the synthesis of relating to the sound system of things and thoughts your environment provides. And later communicating these sounds to other human beings. Finally acquiring and learning your first language. This however shows that humans are organically linguist, from a very nascent stage of life.

Reinventing yourself later in life is not a bad idea after all. It will have beneficial implications in practicality considering each and every aspect of your social life.

How Can You Learn A Language Faster?

A second language learning process can be speedy, if you choose the right language. The final choice will however vary from one person to another. But in general, learning Spanish if you already know English could be far easier for you to learn than to learn Mandarin. But that would not be a valid reason for not learning Mandarin! In fact, it could be your loss. But we will come to discussing that part later in this book.

Remember learning a language is like learning a new sport. If you have played water polo, learning something alike as handball will be comparatively easier for you. Learning a new sport like golf which has different coordination methods could be little more challenging, but never say never! With practice anything is possible.

This advice does not imply that you should never learn a new language from a different language family. On the contrary, the whole objective of this book is to inspire you to climb out of your comfort zone. Just developing a passion for language learning will take care of all the hurdles on the way. Who knows, it could be the most exciting and rewarding journey you would have ever taken in your life!

Bon voyage!

CHAPTER
Three

Carry the World in Your Pocket!

"Learning another language is not only learning different words for the same things, but learning another way to think about things."

—Flora Lewis

Language is something that is extracted from feelings. As Lewis states if you learn different words you will be aware of 'another way to think about things.' How other sect of people feel about those words.

During the time of Facebook, Twitter and the World Wide Web we happen to be interacting with people across borders, 24/7. That's how super connected we are today. This connect is fast-paced and so is life. Business meetings and personal chats happen on Skype. Life is 'on the go' and is highly demanding.

Today, you are competing with candidates from around the world, not just in your country. To cut through the chase, you have to be super awesome. Surely you have to have some skills which are truly useful. Knowledge of different languages is one of those skills, you can bet on.

Everybody's Cup of Tea

- A major chunk of the world's population is either bilingual or multilingual.

- As per numbers quoted in Stavenhagen (1990), five to eight thousand different ethnic groups reside in almost 160 nation states.

- There are roughly more than 5000 distinct languages spoken in 5000 different nation states.

- There are very few mono-ethnic countries in the world.

Learning a new language will be give you better understanding of the interconnections between people of different cultures. The magic about words is that the same or similar words can carry different meanings in different languages. Isn't that astounding!

Most of the time we choose or try to interact with people who speak the same language. It is a very obvious thing to do. It assures familiarity which guarantees comfort and security. We also tend to think that there will always be a better connection with people speaking the same language or at least sharing a similar background. On the surface, this sounds like a very practical way of thinking, but this is self-delusion.

Now imagine being able to crack a big deal overseas only because you knew your business associate's language and could discuss all the project nitty-gritties with him in detail like a native. Or the thrill of making a special friend on a journey abroad, only because you happened to know his/her language! Human exchange of any kind can have a deeper impact with the help of a language. One can not only experience the culture and traditions of a place, if you are able to comprehend the emotions behind it. Multilinguals, are naturally abled to swiftly modify their conduct, as per the language they happen to be speaking in. Skilled linguists automatically become more aware and sensitive to others' needs while reacting to the spoken environment, they find themselves in.

Language speaks for itself. Language is the soul in a culture's oral history. It unveils the centuries-old ideologies. That is the reason why a story written in Sanskrit will not be able to elicit identical influences and emotional ripples when translated and read in English. For instance, the true essence of Mahabharata cannot be captured in English.

To be able to truly appreciate another's cultures and to transcend business across borders, you have to overcome the linguist barrier. To further your career, you have to familiarize yourself with languages other than your mother tongue. If culture shapes your world-view, language gives expression to it.

Give Yourself the Edge

Bilingualism and multilingualism gives a decided edge to a person professionally and personally. Any business project that involves travelling abroad, will throw you up as the first choice, if you knew the language of that country.

"Language matters on a large-scale national level and at the level of smaller businesses," says Gabrielle Hogan-Brun, a research fellow in Language Studies at the University of Bristol. Gabrielle cites interesting data associating languages with economic prosperity.

Let's take the case of Switzerland, a country that credits 10% of its GDP growth to its multilingual legacy. It has four languages used extensively, across the tiny nation: German, French, Italian and a classic Latin-based language called Romansh.

In contrast, Britain attributes only 3.5% of its yearly G.D.P because of its people's poor language aptitude.

As our world becomes more and more connected through technological advances, it's becoming increasingly obvious that learning several languages is a bonus for multiple reasons.

Our world has already shrunk in size. We are talking about the universe of international cuisine. People are opting for home stay while holidaying, in order to experience a new culture. Culture exchange programs in universities across the globe are so common these days.

You would be living under a rock if you disvalue the strength of multilingualism. Language is the simplest way to dive deep into other cultures and seize the global opportunities on offer. In the bargain, who knows you might also discover a few new things to add to your own inner world!

Learn the Hack to Learn Any Language Faster

Just like to learn swimming, you have to first dive in and do it. Similarly learning a new language can only be done by using it as often as possible in your everyday verbal exchange.

Use the language when you are around native speakers so that even if you goof up, there is somebody at hand to immediately correct you.

'Speak the language' --- is the hack that will pull you through.

Things to help you speak the language

- Join a language exchange program
- Be a part of local city language meets
- Ask help from a friend who knows the language
- Hire a private language coach

CHAPTER
Four

A Linguist Will Always Stay A Step Ahead

"You live a new life for every language you speak. If you know only one language, you live only once."

—A Czech proverb

Language reflects a way of life. It reflects how you think, what you think. Indeed, a new language is a new belief system; a new thought process.

The billionaire co-founder of Microsoft, Bill Gates once declared to the assembled media persons that if there is one thing he is utterly disappointed about in life, it's not learning a second language. He professed the wish to know French, Arabic or Chinese and regrets not finding the time to do it. Even he realizes the strategic significance of bilingualism in today's global market.

In a global village, the language connect is very important to flourish in any business that runs operations beyond a country's geographic borders.

There have been studies that prove that workers in Florida, who are fluent in both Spanish and English draw $7000 more per annum than those who only know English. As per a Canadian study, bilingual men and women earn 3.6% and 6.6% respectively, i.e. more in comparison to their only English-speaking counterparts.

How to Learn A Second Language Faster

Here are a few time-tested techniques that I've often used with my students, whom I teach Mandarin.

Weave in your burnout points into the language target sets-

Set simple goals for yourself woven into your daily tasks:

I will not snap at people instantly.

I will eat right.

I will learn Chinese for an hour every day.

If running and music helps you relax, listen to songs in the second language. Even if you are unable to understand the lyrics, you would still enjoy the rhythm and music. Also get accustomed to its tone and words. Run your language!

At Bhaktivedanta Manor Watford, UK

At, IMN Meet, Mumbai, India

CHAPTER
Five

Demystifying Cultural With Language

"Language is the road map of a culture. It tells you where its people come from and where they are going."

—Rita Mae Brown

Language and culture are so intricately interlinked that these days there is a separate, science based, literature discipline - Linguistic anthropology that scientifically evaluates how language impacts our social life.

A language is not just a string of alphabets, word placement and grammar. There is a subtle cultural context embedded in a language. There is a whole science and history to why a word can be placed only at a particular place in a sentence to convey a meaningful thought. It also includes norms and behavior, rituals and customs – in short, everything that makes up the culture of a community.

Let me illustrate this with a film title. Take for instance, *Eternal Sunshine of the Spotless Mind*. If you do a literal translation from its Italian title, it would turn out to be – *If You Leave Me, I Delete*

You. Without context, a language does not convey, the full force of a cultural identity.

Let me relate a different personal experience here. I once travelled to the Amazon rain forest in Colombia. We trekked through the treacherous jungle for a full day. Towards the fag end, we reached a 'Maloca' meaning in local dialect, a conservative town hall for gifted people.

The 'Abuelo' (chief) invited us to a local feast. As the 'Abuelo' talked to us about his tribe's traditions, customs and beliefs, with the help of a smattering of Spanish, that three of us in the group knew, we could strike a rapport with the tribesmen. Eventually, it turned out to be an enriching experience for all of us. Language is the vehicle for the culture, philosophy and spirit of a region.

Linguistic Relativity

The Theory of Linguistic Relativity says that the language you use to discuss the world has a direct effect on the way you would continue to think about the world. Linguist and Anthropologist Edward Sapir says the language speaking habits of groups vastly differ and that's what makes them unique and the only way to connect with a person from a different culture is through his/her language.

Make Language Learning A Part of Your Daily Timetable

Don't just set priorities but also have a schedule to meet those priorities. Past research has shown, that setting aside a fixed time of the day for language learning is the most productive method.

Here are a few practical suggestions on how to rake in more language time into your daily routine:

1. Cutting down on your work time: Meaning if you have set a deadline of two hours for the task, reduce it to one hour, and devote the second hour to second/new language learning.

2. Cut down on your time spend on social media activities: Instead of checking your mails five times a day, do it twice and use the balance time for language learning.

3. Club these two activities into one slot –This technique however is not advisable for

important tasks, because multi-tasking can often lead to multi-trashing.

Last but not the least, cut down on your sleep time: Minus-ing half an hour sleep to devote it to language learning will not make you a loser. Contrarily, it will earn you the epitaph of an accomplished linguist. Go for it.

CHAPTER
Six

Mandarin – A Mantra for the Multicultural World

"Learn everything you can, anytime you can, from anyone you can; there will always come a time when you will be grateful you did."

—Sarah Caldwell

Let me reveal a small secret to you. These days, Mandarin has risen to become Australia's second language, after English!

Every year, on April 20, the United Nations celebrate the World Chinese Language Day. This is "to celebrate multilingualism and cultural diversity as well as to promote equal use of all six official languages throughout the organization," declares the UN.

The most spoken language in the world

With roughly 1.2 billion speaking the Chinese language, it's arguably the world's most widely spoken languages. You'll find Chinese speakers anywhere and everywhere. Indeed, they outnumber English language speakers in the ratio of 2:1.

China currently has the world's 2nd largest Gross Domestic Product

Economists predict that by 2040, China will overtake the US (and the EU) as the world's biggest economy. This would undoubtedly make the learning of Mandarin imperative for business growth anywhere in the world. According to the National Bureau of Statistics of China, the country's economy was seven times larger in 2015 than it was in 2000, and it continues to grow at the same meteoric rate.

Chinese businessmen and women are now spread throughout the world, and learning Mandarin is the perfect way to connect and do business with them.

In addition to approximately 1.4 billion Chinese living in China, there are also more than 50,000,000 overseas Chinese (regardless of citizenship) mostly living in Southeast Asia and in significant numbers in the US, UK, Peru, South Korea and Australia. Counted together, they make up for 20% of the world's population. A few large US cities, such as San Francisco claim about 21% population of Chinese descent. And they don't live in shanties called "Chinatowns" – they have moved upwards to satellite towns. The Chinese diaspora have taken the world by storm.

Why Chinese of All Language?

According to Bloomberg, as of November 2017, the Chinese economy is projected to overtake the United States economy in 2028 and has the potential of challenging the supremacy of English especially in business circles as China pips the United States out of the top spot as the nation with the world's highest GDP. Meaning, if you want to work in international trade and the digital market, then you should really think about learning Chinese as China's digital market is presently the largest today. Although known for being challenging to learn, knowing Chinese pays dividends as China is truly transcending globally.

Its Mark Zuckerberg's second language too!

I read in the newspapers that Facebook founder Mark Zuckerberg spoke in Chinese during a Q&A

session at Tsinghua University in China recently. The audience was undoubtedly floored at his command over the language. He is not alone. CEOs across the business world have taken to Chinese as their second language.

Chinese students make up a third of the international student community in the US universities

They are the largest community on US campuses, followed by the Indian community. So, whether you are enrolled in a home university or studying abroad, you are bound to come into contact with Chinese international students on campus as classmates, friends and fellow students.

A useful language for the future

A recently survey[1] done by the British Council showed that British parents want their wards to select Chinese as their second non-European

---

[1]UK parents: Mandarin 'most beneficial' non-European language, Thursday 05 January 2017, https://www.britishcouncil.org/contact/press/uk-parents-mandarin-most-beneficial-non-european-language

language over French, Spanish or Japanese as 'the most useful language for the future." **UK parents saw Mandarin (Chinese) as the 'most beneficial' non-European language for their children to learn, according to the BC research released as part of the Mandarin Excellence Program, launched by the British Council in September in 2016.**

Among the parents, nearly five per cent of those surveyed picked Chinese language in their top three when asked which languages they thought would be most valuable for their child's future.

When questioned specifically about Mandarin, more than half (51 per cent) of the British parents said they thought that learning the language would boost their children's career prospects while 56 per cent saw it as a skill that would open their children's minds to an 'exciting and dynamic' culture. A similar number (51 per cent) stated that they would like their children to have the opportunity to study Mandarin, with more than a quarter (27 per cent) saying that they would actively be encouraging their children to learn the language.

And while the more traditional languages French, Spanish and German were favourites overall (picked in the top three by 57 per cent, 54 per cent and 40 per cent of parents respectively), Mandarin was considered the most vital non-European language for young people in the UK to speak – well-ahead of Arabic and Japanese (both 14 per cent).

With the whole world bullish about the Chinese economy, it's very likely that the Chinese language will begin to enter more classrooms in foreign countries, as the years go by.

Language Hack to Learn Chinese Faster

I as a practicing Chinese language teacher know that among all foreign languages, this language has a relatively uncomplicated grammar and syntax structure. Unlike French, German or English, Chinese has no verb conjugation, hence no need to memorize verbs and tenses!

Additionally, as our Bangla language, Mandarin also does not have any noun declension (e.g., gender and number distinctions). In English, a new learner often gets confused with the use of different verb forms such as "see/saw/seen." In Chinese you just have to remember one word: *kan* for the same usage. Likewise, while in English you have to distinguish between "cat" and "cats," in Chinese there is only one form: *mao*.

However, that doesn't make the language any simplistic for the Chinese have devised other ways of conveying these distinctions in tenses and numbers. But it would be correct to say that you don't have to worry about verbs! And as there are no verbs, no plurals, no tenses, no subject-verb agreement, and no conjugations, your job, as a learner becomes all easier.

Best of all, of the voluminous 80,000 Chinese characters only 3,500 are used in general practice, so you can banish the rest!

CHAPTER
Seven

A Guide to Learn Mandarin Quickly

"There are no limitations to the mind except those we acknowledge."

—Napoleon Hill

Tell me honestly - do you really really, need me to give you a huge practical reason to learn a foreign language?

Spoken language is such a powerful communicative tool between two or more persons that you don't need another raison d'être to learn a language. If Mandarin is your choice of a foreign language, I would say, "Why not?" and ask you to go let your heart feel the language, embrace it, and then just learn it! However, before you take the plunge:

Do your basic research

There is a Chinese saying, "磨刀不误砍柴工", which upon translation means "the more the preparation, the faster work gets done." There may be thousands of articles and video tutorials on the internet which may claim, to make you learn the

Chinese language in flat 30-days or less, but don't let yourself be lured. You should read up about the people and culture who speak that language to determine if you would indeed want to master it as your second tongue.

Celebrity Mandarin Learners

Other than Facebook CEO & Founder Mark Zuckerberg Australian Prime Minister Kevin Rudd and former US Treasury Secretary Timothy Geithner also studied Chinese at Beijing University. Prince William also gave an interview in Mandarin recently, as he wished everybody a Happy Chinese New Year!

Other than this, in case of the Chinese language, a few basic questions that you need to ask yourself could be:

- Do I need to learn both simple and complex Chines characters?

- Why are Chinese characters made of strokes and not letters?

- What is the history behind this practice?

- What is the difference between Mandarin and Cantonese?

- Which one should I choose?

- Who should I choose as my teacher?

- How long would it take for me to master the language?

- What is the definition of 'language proficiency'?

- How many hours should I devote in a day to my language practice?

- What offline and online resources can I tap into to improve my practice?

Listen before you speak

Let your ears get used to the phonetics. Sound training is very important, to any language learning process. Read language passages to yourself. Using a phonetic writing system, such as Pinyin, you would soon get used to the sounds you would be hearing.

Learning the alphabets and characters is equally important. But in my experience and training as a student, initially, getting familiar with phonetics is most important in language learning. Then when you are accustomed to the sound elements you can get on with learning the characters and pick up a little momentum in your language learning process.

Students who do otherwise, I have experienced, easily get intimidated with the look of the Chinese characters. I admit, Chinese characters do look somewhat complex, like the characters of Urdu language, but with persistent practice and patience, learners can get a hang of both the scripts.

Otherwise also, it's rather far-fetched to get a sense of the characters, without knowing what they may sound like; what meaning they produce when strung together in a sentence; or how different Chinese words and phrases work together, to produce a meaningful dialogue.

A new language can sound a lot like undifferentiated noise in the beginning. But give yourself time and soak in all the unfamiliar sounds before you get on with the character differentiation. Let your brain register the sounds, before you ask it to recognize the shapes of the characters. In my experience, aural cues always get processes faster than visual cues and there must be a scientific reason for that.

Memorizing characters daily

Once you decide to study Chinese characters, work on them every day. Devote half an hour to an hour a day, just on learning characters. Use whatever method you want, but set aside dedicated character learning time every day. Why every day? Because you will forget the characters almost as quickly as you learn them and therefore need to relearn them again and again.

Cast aside the rule book. Go with pattern recognition

Focus on patterns. Don't get caught up in complicated grammar explanations, just focus on patterns. It is better to get used to the patterns that Chinese uses, to express things we express in English, using English patterns. Chinese has rather uncomplicated grammar, one of the pleasures of learning Chinese. There are no declensions, conjugations, genders, verb aspects, complicated tenses or other sources of confusion that are found in many European languages.

Become a voracious reader

Read a lot. This is much easier to do today. You can find material on the internet, use online dictionaries and apps like LingQ. It has not only special texts for learners, but even a wide range of material on subjects of interest to you.

Practice makes a man or a woman perfect

You will need to practice a lot, both speaking to yourself and speaking to others. Practice imitating, what you are listening to. Find texts for which you have the audio. Listen to a phrase or sentence and then try to imitate the intonation, without worrying too much about individual sounds. You may even want to record yourself to compare. If you can get "infected" with the rhythm of the language, not only will your control of tones improve, but your choice of words will also become more native like.

When you speak, don't second guess yourself on tones, or any other aspect of the language. Just let the words and phrases you have heard and practiced, flow out, even with the mistakes and all. Every time you use the language, you are practicing and getting used to it. If you enjoy interacting in Chinese, if you enjoy getting in the flow, singing to the rhythm, then your Mandarin will continue to improve.

Remember that you already have the superpowers within to make your mark in the world, so use that power to learn Chinese on your own—and enjoy the journey!

Language Hack to Learn Any Language Faster

This one is absolutely for the beginners.

The very first word to learn in Chinese is "xièxie" 谢谢, i.e. "Thanks" in English but I've found that it's actually a very hard word to pronounce, especially for beginners.

Therefore, here's a quick easy way to learn the word.

Try pronouncing it in rhyme with the English word "share" but try this with a serious Boston accent. Please don't laugh. Just recall how Ben Affleck speaks in *Good Will Hunting*. He uses a deadly Boston accent. Acquire that in front of your mirror.

Seriously, it works! Just give it a try!

CHAPTER
Eight

Learn Thai,
The Thai Way

"If one could read fluently, confidently, in every known language, one would have no need of translators or translations; one could read Homer on Mondays, Akhmatova on Tuesdays, Swahili poets on Wednesdays, and so on."

—Abraham Verghese,
Cutting for Stone

Thai is spoken by nearly 60 million people in Thailand, neighboring countries and across the world. Based on personal experience, here are six reasons why I would recommend Thai language to everyone.

Why Pick Thai?

It's a native language, to over 50 million people worldwide in Thailand and neighboring countries, such as Laos and Burma. Thailand is an exciting and exotic country that draws millions of tourists from across the globe each year. Known for its sandy beaches, lush green rain forests, wildlife and lofty mountains, many throng its shores each year.

You will make inroads into the beautiful Thai culture

Armed with the knowledge, even a smattering of Thai will transform your experience of that country. You can then easily soak into its rich and varied cultural and literary tradition.

Learning to read Thai may initially turn out to be a long and arduous process but in the end, it's well worth the rewards. For instance, the way Thai address each other; the quaint colloquialisms they use; the way they differentiate and classify various objects, is so different, just wading through the myriad phrases will make you appreciate their cultural nuances. Example, *grengjai (being gracious), mai pen rai (never mind/it's ok/no problem), even som nom na (serves you right) are so typically Thai or Thai style that you would be charmed off your feet, by their polite manner.*

Additionally, you will begin to appreciate, typical cultural practices like, in Thailand it's okay to *refer to someone's child as your own (luuk), or lok son dua is equivalent to the declaration that "I am happy with my own company."* I am sure, you get the drift. Language is the best means to incorporate a little bit of Thai charm in your behavior and mannerism; make friends with them and understand their local dialect.

Find a job in Thailand

Believe me, Thai are very hospitable people. The economy is booming and several Thai companies, ranging from education to realty to financial services are actively looking to hire expats who can converse in their language. Even their school system is quite similar to the Indian system, so there could be vacancies for good English-speaking teachers of Indian origin in those schools. Your knowledge of Thai will certainly give you an edge in education, service sector or business. I've been given to understand that presently, Thai to English translators are in very high demand, both in governmental offices and the private sector. The hospitality sector also prefers to get on board multilingual staff that are fluent in several languages and can easily build a rapport with the overseas guests.

Your travel to Thailand will be a lot more fun

Imagine travelling to Thailand and being able to read all street signs and directions; make small talk with the receptionist at your hotel's travel desk and speaking Thai to the driver of the Tuk Tuk! Can you visualize the look of surprise that would flash on the driver's face?

Also imagine how easy it would be for you to be able to read the restaurant menus at many of the local eateries. This is not to say that, without the knowledge of the local language, you will find yourself completely at a loss in Thailand. Reason; many Thais speak very good English, but the experience won't match that of traveler who can converse in the local dialect.

Learning Thai has been a hugely fascinating and personally rewarding experience for me. In learning this language, I've observed similarities with various other languages I know. In particular, my knowledge of Chinese has proven to be extremely useful, in terms of shared vocabulary, tones, and grammatical points of reference.

Let me confess - I've been told I speak with a decent Chinese accent when I speak Thai, which frankly, was a revelation to me! During the course of my learning, I also found vocabulary words that are common, would you believe it in Arabic, Japanese and Thai! Three regions of the world that are so far apart in distance from each other?

I admit that given my existing knowledge of Asian languages, it may be difficult for me to be completely objective about, assessing the difficulty of Thai. But let me confess this --- The basic structure and syntax of Thai is simple and straightforward. You can very quickly pick up a basic working knowledge of the language and start conversing in it, rest assured.

While learning Thai language, I learnt the Thai culture and it became an enriching lingual experience

As I immersed myself in learning the Thai language, the curious 'me,' simultaneously went on to read a battery of books on the rich Thai culture and religion. On this journey, I leant the finer nuances of the language. Earlier I just knew the words but now 'I literally discovered' the cultural connotations to several of those words.

This was undoubtedly an intellectually stimulating process which I whole heartedly enjoyed. After this, I had a better and broader understanding of the Thai world and some of my previously-held misconceptions got shattered. For instance, earlier I carried the impression that India is the only country which follows the tradition of having extended families. I was wrong. The Thais also have a very closely-knit extended family culture.

Traditionally, each generation maintains a deep connect with first, second and even third cousins. Indeed, would you believe it that the Thais do not have an equivalent word for 'cousins.' They address each other as brothers and sisters in Thai language.

An observation here --- my mother tongue is Gujarati and we also don't have an equivalent word for cousins. It's either 'Bhai' or 'Ben', meaning brother or sister. It's the same clannish culture I observed in Thailand.

In order to keep the bond alive with the extended family members, Thai prefer to live close to each other in family clusters. Even when they leave their village for work opportunities, they don't forget their roots. In a situation where the parents have to leave their house to go out to seek work, there are always uncles, aunts and grandparents to take care of the children. This, as we all know is a very uncommon practice in the Western societies.

'The concept of face' is crucial in Thailand. It represents dignity/ respect and shame/disrespect. It stands for 'saving face' and 'loosing face' respectively. The thought behind this is, one should not disrespect the other. This attitude is important keep negativity at a bay.

Another notable practice is to carry a token gift whenever you drop by at someone's place. You must also leave your shoes outside the house. You cannot forget the universal greeting 'Wai' with folded hands in a prayerful manner, as we Indians do, except that the Thai also bow down a little indicating courtesy and respect for the other.

All this is called 'saving face'. Criticism, shouting at someone in the presence of other people is considered 'loosing face'. Fundamentally, a person rises in esteem of others by good deeds and actions and polite forms of behaviour. The idea is to create and maintain harmony at all costs and avoid feuds of all kind.

A public show of unrestraint anger, outbursts, display of rage, crying out in a public place is frowned upon in their culture. These feelings aren't ignored though, these are dealt with in a more mature and private manner. It's just that Thais don't want their emotions to be exposed to all and 'loose face' in the crowd. No wonder, Thais are generally considered as nonchalant people, due of this particular tradition.

The Thai spirit is also ingrained with a feeling of honour for the nation. They take pride in the fact that their country is the only country in the whole of Southeast Asia, which was not colonised by the British.

I have always wondered about this charming tourism tagline associated with Thailand: 'Land of smiles.' As I did my reading bit on Thailand, I realised that smile is not a 'smile' in its truest sense in Thailand. A smile is sometimes used as a cover up as well. Since you cannot betray any negative emotional outburst in public, so even when Thais are hurt or unhappy, they must always smile. This bit of façade, however does not take away any bit of hospitability, warmth and genuine goodness of the people. The smile aspect is a way living, it is how their culture flourishes and their society functions.

No, is a big word for the Thai people. They practically avoid using the word in even the most trying of situations. So, if a Thai says an outright 'No' to you on an occasion, it must mean something is drastically wrong! 'Maybe' is their choice of expression, which at times genuinely means, maybe, most of the times it's a substitute for point right 'NO.'

On the flip side, 'yes' is not factually, 'yes.' They will say 'yes' to things they don't want to commit to, Thais don't believe in putting down other people or dashing someone's expectations. Denial is impolite. Schedules are flexible and the desire to please all is overarching

The primary religion practised in Thailand is Buddhism, precisely, Theravada Buddhism. The religious traditions followed here, are much more distinct than any other Buddhist country. They also imbibe exterior components, which are more inclusive in nature. For instance, Thais believe in the existence of souls and spirits, contrary to the standard Buddhist belief.

Superstitions with regards to ghosts and evil spirits prevail, even among the educated, city-bred people. It is a conventional to consult a psychic or a monk to pick the right date for the celebration of any auspicious event. Buying a new house, a wedding, a car test drive, will always be done on a chosen auspicious day, in consultation with the monk.

Talking about monks, they are held in high esteem in the society. Again, unlike other Asian cultures, in Thailand, priests or monks are not confined to churches or temples you will virtually find them all over the place – strolling on the roads, on your bus travels, partaking in festivities and other day to day, commonplace scenarios. As you run into monks in the commonest of settings, even a slightest disregard of other people, is out of question.

Ironically however, bodily consciousness is a virtue that all Thais swear by. Each part of the human body has a certain degree of value attached to it, culturally. Head is considered to be highly sacred and most respected. A friendly pat on the head, as a prank or even lovingly running your hands through children's hair is considered downright insulting.

The feet on the other hand are not so revered part of the human body. Indeed feet are deemed as downright filthy. Don't ever use any foot touch gesture, when in Thailand. Never sit with your foot sole pointed outside another person or pointing at an image of the Buddha. Some Thai also take offence if you cross your legs. Further, do not open doors, move your bag or do any such activity with your feet instead of using your outstretched hand. At most places remain prepared to remove your foot wear.

All this may appear quirky to an outsider but for the Thai it's mundane and expected. But don't fret or worry if you are initially slow at picking up these cultural nuances. Thai are super understanding and friendly with tourists. They are a very tolerant lot.

Still don't risk offending a Thai by being sarcastic about their religion or monarchy, resorting to public screaming, and walking the street in semi naked state. You will shock these mild folks out of their wits.

My visit to Thailand opened a window to a new way of living on this planet. I found remarkably similar tones and overtones with my Hindu culture and philosophy, but also sensed the dissimilarities. To illustrate, we also consider the head region as sacred. We remove shoes and cover our heads during a temple visit. These points of convergence made me feel like a kindred soul and blur the lines of differences.

Language Hack to Learn Any Language Faster

Languages, indeed all languages carry, tens of thousands of words but, only a limited number of these get used in our daily practice. Actually, that's all you need anyways to be able to converse in that language. However, remember the use of the Pareto Principle, also known as the 80/20 rule. Put in 20% effort and I assure you, you can expect 80% gains.

This is especially valid for Thai language. Its grammar is extremely simple. Just make sure you string together the words in right order, and your pronunciation is ok and wait and see how it works!

CHAPTER
Nine

Language Learning and the Young Generation

"If you talk to a man in a language he understands, that goes to his head. If you talk to him in his own language, that goes to his heart."

—Nelson Mandela

It's a busy autumn morning at the Spanish Nursery, a bilingual nursery school in north London. As the school is about to commence, parents help their toddlers out of cycling helmets and jackets. Teachers greet them with a cheerful, "Buenos dias!"In the playground, a little girl asks for her hair to be bunched up into a "coleta" (Spanish for 'pigtail'), then sends a ball rolling on the ground and enthusiastically yells, "catch!" in English.

"At this age, children don't learn a language – they simply acquire it," the school's director Carmen Rampersad told the BBC correspondent Sophie Hardach.[1]

---

[1] Sophie Hardach, What is the best age to learn a language, BBC Future, http://www.bbc.com/future/story/20181024-the-best-age-to-learn-a-foreign-language

This sentence effectively sums up the effortlessness required in teaching a new language to children. For these children profiled by the BBC, Spanish happens to be a third or sometimes, a fourth language, after their mother tongues, which may include Croatian, Hebrew, Korean and Dutch.

In the article, *The Mystery of People Who Speak Dozens of Languages*, the New Yorker journalist Judith Thurman writes[2], he recounts how Ezzofanti, the son of a carpenter, picked up Latin just by standing outside a seminary, listening to the boys recite their conjugations.

Likewise, Rojas-Berscia, the son of a Peruvian businessman, who grew up in an educated trilingual household and lived a privileged life in Lima learnt to speak Piedmontese from his grandmother. He learnt Italian from his mother of Italian origin and English in preschool. The boy developed such a keen interest in foreign languages that along with Maltese, he wants to learn to speak well in Uighur and Sanskrit.

---

[2]Judith Thurman, https://www.newyorker.com/magazine/2018/09/03/the-mystery-of-people-who-speak-dozens-of-languages, August 27, 2018

Asked where and how he picked up his love for the languages, he told the New Yorker journalist that he developed it over a dinner at a Chinese restaurant in Nijmegen, where he was chatting in Mandarin with the owner and in Dutch with a server, while alternating between French and Spanish with a fellow-student at the institute. "I'm an *amoureux de langues*. And, when I fall in love with a language, I have to learn it. There's no practical motive—it's a form of play." An *amoureux* in French is a lover, and this boy described himself as a lover of languages.

My own love affair with foreign languages (I speak four), may be nothing to boast about in those parts of the world, where multilingualism is the norm, but in India, I still raise eyebrows. People who straddle various cultures, say Melanesians, South Asians, Latin-Americans, Central Europeans, sub-Saharan Africans, namely the Maltese and the Shawis, I have noticed acquire languages, as a matter of habit, without considering it as a super achievement.

"On my way to the Netherlands, I once overheard a Ghanaian taxi-driver chatting on his cell phone in a language that I immediately didn't recognize. "It's Hausa," he confessed in me later," a blogger once recounted on www.Languagechat[3].

Bilingualism Impacts Brain Development

A fascinating article in The New York Times explains the ways in which the brains of babies in bilingual households develop differently from those raised in a mono-lingual household. Apparently, while bilingual babies take longer to distinguish phonetic sounds in either language, once they do come to recognize them, they can then hear them in both languages, while mono-lingual babies lose this facility by the time they are one. Even in the womb, one study showed that babies born to bilingual mothers not only prefer both of those languages over others — but are also able to register that the two languages are different. Wow!

"I speak in it with my father, whose family comes from Nigeria. But I speak Twi with my mom, Ga with my friends, some Ewe, and English

____

[3]Maltese for Beginners, language chat, http://languagehat.com/maltese-for-beginners/

is our lingua franca." Linguistically speaking, that taxi-driver is a more typical citizen of the globe than an average American, the blogger feels.

Take the case of Adul Sam-on, one of the teen-age soccer players rescued, last July from a cave in Mae Sai in Thailand[4]. Adul grew up in abject poverty in Thailand, on the border of Myanmar and Laos, also got exposed to all the three cultures. His family belonged to an ethnic minority, the Wa, who spoke an Austroasiatic language that is widely used in parts of China. In addition to WA, according to *The New York Times*, Adult is "proficient" in Thai, Burmese, Mandarin, and English—which enabled him to interpret for the two British divers who discovered the trapped team."

Learning a foreign language helps children see the world with an altogether different perspective, leading to a problem-solving approach in all challenges they encounter, later in life. The ability to consider multiple viewpoints facilitates creative problem solving.

---

[4]Megan Specia, Want to know more about the trapped Thai boys, The New York Times, https://www.nytimes.com/2018/07/06/world/asia/what-to-know-about-the-trapped-thai-boys.html, July 6, 2018

Learn Mandarin and you can effectively converse with over a billion people, across the world. Learn Hindi and you can engage with another 650 million! Spanish can put another 420 million in your friends' circuit. And if you already know English, you could be speaking to nearly half the world's population!

While English has become the lingua franca of the world, learning a foreign language (or two) increases a plethora of business opportunities and opens the door to all the benefits of multilingualism.

Benefits of Learning a Foreign Language as a child

Catch them young is the advice I give to most parents.

Give Them a Head Start

Past research indicates that children, who pick a second language before the age of five, learn it at a much faster pace, as their brain is already linguistically conditioned. In addition, young learners are uninhibited and enthusiastic, which adult learners often are not.

Start Early, Late Ending

Past studies have also found that the age at which you start learning a second language has a direct and positive impact on a child's intellectual wave length. It matures them faster.

Food For Thought

Research shows that learning a second language boosts problem-solving, critical-thinking and listening skills, in addition to improving memory, concentration, and the ability to multitask. Children proficient in several languages show remarkable mental agility.

Pushes Up Their IQ

It's also been observed that knowledge of multiple languages, helps in a child's academic performance. Such children report improved reading, writing, and math skills, generally score higher in all academic tests.

Triggers Intrigue, Cultural Compatibility Pluralism and Empathy

Children who get exposed to foreign languages are more understanding of other cultural practices and grow up as progressive, tolerant global citizens.

Age No Bar

While it's recommended to start young, with training and the use of specific learning techniques, even an adult brain can be taught to learn a new language. These are the findings of a study done at University College London, where it was found that the difficulties that adults report in learning languages do not have any biological basis. It's just an inhibition in the mind. Given the right teacher, material and environment, even adults can be as responsive to language stimuli as child language learners.

Go for Two... or Three

Contrary to popular belief, young children do not get or feel overburdened with the learning of multiple languages. On the contrary, they are natively (or naturally) multilingual and take to a new language as fish takes to water.

What Role Can You Play as a Parent?

Whether you belong to a multi-cultural, bilingual family or not, your support to your child will make tremendous difference as to his/her learning of a new language. Indeed, it is not necessary to be fluent in the language your child is learning, in order to offer a supportive, learning environment. Gentle encouragement and a reassuring attitude, will more than suffice.

In Sum...

No matter what your age, learning a foreign language will make you a seasoned global citizen. It will strengthen and establish new neutral pathways. It can increase your confidence in dealing with a pluralistic world and instill in you, a deep sense of empathy for others.

CHAPTER
Ten

My Shanghai-Quzhou Diary

This chapter is devoted to a few fond memories of my trip to Shanghai and Quzhou around Diwali in 2018

It was a sixteen days educational trip organised by the Chinese consular, Mumbai. We were a happy bunch of teachers from Mumbai and Pune, set to attend a teacher's training session in these two Chinese cities. We were also accomplished Mandarin trainers.

In Shanghai we received further training in the lingua franca of the region, from native Mandarin, who took our teaching of Chinese to a different level of expertise, altogether. In between the language training sessions at East China Normal University (ECNU) Shanghai, we also learned Taichi, which is a Chinese physical exercise technique marked by deliberately slow, very focussed, movements that is both physically and mentally relaxing. Just as Yoga is hugely popular in India, Taichi art is a very ancient and popular performing art form in mainland China.

Chinese Opera at Quzhou

Our Chinese instructor (addressed respectfully as 'Master') explained that Taichi is so blissful, you feel like sleeping afterwards. From him, we learnt different positions of Taichi and the name of each.

At these sessions, the instructor took us through the history of Taichi Fan Tiao, a martial art dance form, which is also a meditative technique. Some of the most famous positions in the Chinese culture are: The Golden Peacock and the Huashan Mountain. In addition, on this fun-filled visit, we learnt the art of paper-cutting arts and also visited the library inside the ECNU campus.

Although some of these Taichi positions were complex and required complete control of body limbs, it was fun practicing Taichi at the sprawling, breezy ECNU Garden.

We observed during our stay at Quzhou that the villagers live a spartan life of frugal means and they work very hard. Almost everything they do, they do manually, such as washing clothes in the river, ploughing the fields etc. The Chinese women work shoulder-to-shoulder with the men folk and often women far outnumber the men in all spheres, including ploughing fields, operating heavy machinery and retailing garments at mega malls. We witnessed women empowerment everywhere.

The liveliest sight was the wall paintings on village hutments in Quzhou and Kecheng – brought to life with motifs of animals, flowers and birds etc., just like the Warli paintings in Gujarat villages. We visited Yu Dong village and our hearts felt warmed with the hospitality received from our hosts.

Confucius Museum at Quzhou, Shanghai

Tea Garden Quzhou, Shanghai

Paper Cutting Art, Learnt at East China Normal University

Root Palace, Museum, Quzhou

Root Palace, Museum, Quzhou

Orange Groove, Quzhou

Oriental Hotel, Quzhou

Medal received at Quzhou Language School

Painting on Rice paper learnt at ECNU, Sanghai

Painting on Rice paper learnt at ECNU, Sanghai

We also noticed that the Chinese villagers sell everything from painting to clothes to silk scarves, besides every other knicks knacks.

Statue of Mao-Tse-Tung at East China Normal University

Calligraphy Brush Store at Shanghai

Mazhang Tribal Games at Quzhou

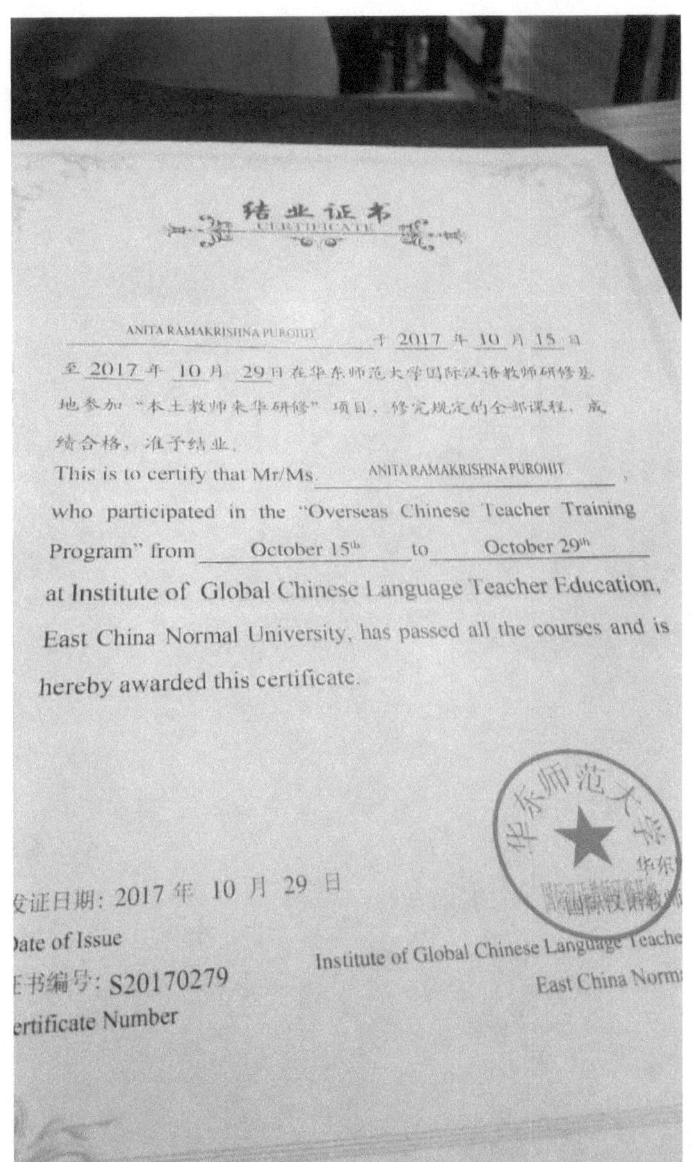

My Training Certificate at East China, Normal University, Shanghai

Tea Garden at Quzhou

ECNU Chinese Class

The Famous Tai-Chi Art at Shanghai

Majiang, a form of gambling is a major leisurely activity of the Quzhou villagers, we were graciously invited to join in. A few of us won and a few lost in the game but it was fun for everybody.

When we went for a tour of China Art Museum, I met Amy, a student volunteer at Hanban, the short form of the Office of Chinese Language Council International in Shanghai, who was assigned to us as our escort. As I trundled out of the museum gate, earlier than the rest, Amy joined me and as I recall, we had a good discussion.

She said that on her next visit to India, she would want to learn Italian from me. In the Department of Hanban teachers' training, I also ran into two young teachers, who had recorded my voice, while I was speaking Chinese. They marvelled at my correct pronunciation of a few difficult words, including YIENDUOREN.

My vegetarian food habits were a major concern there, but not until I voiced it to Linliang, who personally took me to canteen and told the man at the counter to keep 'sucai' (vegetable dishes) aside on a separate table for me to savour.

Despite the imploration of our main escort Dr Upadhyay to speak in Mandarin during the course of our trip, I observed that no one bothered to do so and continued to speak either in English or Marathi. We gifted diyas to the Chinese hotel staff, and they were so curious they wanted to know why I put a 'tilak' on my forehead.

We were all surprised to notice that the Chinese are so hard working; even an average Chinese's standard of living is very high. We didn't notice any signs of extreme poverty in that country.

My best memory is of the extremely polite and courteous people in Quzhou. They have a wonderful sense of hospitality and given a choice, I would like to visit the country several times again!

Summing Up

I feel blessed that all these years, my life's journey has been truly uncommon, rewarding and adventurous.

I completed my M.Sc. in Physics, followed by an M.Phil. in 1987 from Sambalpur University, Orissa. After that, I won a UGC-CSIR Fellowship and chose to do my PhD in Nuclear Physics. Those were the golden years of my life, when all I did was read, read and read. Undistracted by any other thoughts, I turned out to be a brilliant student throughout my career,

In March 1991, I got married against my wishes and that was the turning point of my life. Although married and entrusted with responsibilities, I began to gradually drift away emotionally from my family. I was then a Professor of Physics at

Mumbai University, managing a child at home, giving lectures; and also preparing for GRE and TOEFL& exams. Yet I felt stagnant.

I found a new purpose in 1995, when I took a huge bank loan to establish Purohit Academy, my dream project in Andheri, Mumbai. Today, my day starts and ends at the Academy. I was so consumed in the Academy work that I quit my job at Mumbai University and occupied myself full-time to linguistic training.

I started with Italian and then when I had mastered that language, I started teaching students, mainly corporate executives, businessmen and housewives. During the year 2000, 2001 and 2002, we bagged several corporate contracts for training and translations in different foreign languages. A few of our biggest clients include L & T, Godrej, Lanxess India, Datamatics, Infosys, Syntel, TCS, PCS, and more.

We did extremely well until 2005 – 2006 and I felt very proud about being a 'solo-linguistic entrepreneur' but slowly competition started intensifying in the industry with several fly-by-night operators offering a slew of online courses.

Despite this, we stuck to our time-tested pattern of offline training through seminars, college events and language camps, through our goodwill somehow managed to maintain the same momentum of growth.

These days, life is continuing to move – I would not say turtle's pace but rather at a horse's pace. I would like to quote a famous English poet, Robert Frost's words here: "The woods are lovely, dark and deep, but I have miles to go before I sleep."

These words capture my work ethics, as well.

About the Purohit Academy

Located in Andheri (East), the Purohit Academy (https://purohitacademy.com) founded by Dr. Anita Purohit, is one of the oldest language institute in Mumbai.

Besides language training, the well-appointed, well-staffed institute also provides admission & visa assistance to students keen on pursuing an educational programme in reputed universities in US/UK/Canada.

"Teaching is the profession that teaches all the other professions" says Anita Purohit.

Started in 1995, the Academy has grown into a core hub for language learning, having trained over

5,000 students in various foreign languages. Also we prepare them in GMAT, GRE, TOEFL, SAT, IELTS, TWE, TSE. The alumni of Purohit Academy are spread across the world, either enrolled in the best of universities or employed with reputed corporate entities in India and abroad.

Study Abroad Assistance

- Career counselling and selection of the right course/University

- Pre-requisite for admissions

- Short listing

- Pre-application procedure

- Statement of purpose (SOP)

- Visa guidance

- Facilitating education loans from financial institutes

Presently, the 23-years old Purohit Academy teaches ten foreign languages to students and working professionals- Thai, Japanese, French, Urdu, German, Italian, Arabic, Spanish, Mandarin, and has language trained executives of at least a hundred-odd corporate clients.

Language Courses

Certificate (Basic/Advanced)

Courses Details

- The course covers all three - reading, writing (script) and talking (conversation) sessions.

- The Academy provides all study material to the enrolled student.

- Audio and video aides used extensively in language training.

- At the end of each course the student has to write an exam and a certificate is issued based on his performance.

- Besides language training, the Academy also gives them cultural competency training.

- One can opt for a shorter duration courses also that runs up to a month.

- Along with language training, working professionals are also given soft skill training, how to negotiate and power dress etc.

Why Purohit Academy?

- We provide lots of study and reference materials to our students.

- Conduct a series of mock tests, followed by intensive evaluation and discussions.

- Conduct trial sessions.

- Suggest scientific ways and means of developing analytical thinking.

- Offer a cordial learning atmosphere, where students study in micro groups.

- Provide constructive feedbacks to students to speed up their knowledge and learning.

How We Score

- Damayanti Rawat- SAP professional, RPG LIFE SCIENCE- IELTS general:- 8/9

- Ritesh Doshi Engg. TATADOCOMO-IELTS general:- 7.5/8

- Anirudh Shelkar, BBA student, SYMBIOSIS-Pune, IELTS academic:- 8/9

- Veena D'souza, IELTS general: 7.5/9

- Kavya Naik, IELTS general:8/9

- Kunj Haria, IELTS academic:8/9

- Gopal Borude, IELTS general:8/9

Learning Mandrin A Joy Ride With Us

At Purohit Academy, we have invested a lot of research effort in developing an extensive as well as intensive module in Chinese language; keeping in mind the learning needs of entrepreneurs, business executives, as well students.

Chinese being a tonal language, we focus mainly on tone training, vocabulary building, and correct grammar usage. We help Indians talk to their Chinese business counterparts in terms of practical applications in the present day work scenario.

Our syllabus is systematically organized into two levels of training. At the end of the course, we expect the learner to be able to greet business associates in Chinese language, easily make small talk, place a telephone call, negotiate business terms, not be duped or feel handicapped with his lack of knowledge of the Chinese language etc.

Our syllabus covers all practical aspects to day to day business dealings - numerals, days of the week, months, currency measures, particles, sentence structuring etc. Finally, it also covers common dialogues at various places, drills for self-practice, modes of traveling and going out for shopping etc. in China, i.e. all practical aspects that would make a non-native language competent in China.

Our Top Corporate Clients and the Languages We Taught Them

Clients	Languge Course Offered
Godrej Pillsbury Ltd.	Japanese
Godrej Ltd.	Japanese, Russian
Rajasthan Mills Ltd.	Italian
Real Value	Japanese
Hindustan Electronics	Japanese
Larsen & Toubro	Japanese, Italian
Gidc-Electronics-Gujrat	Japanese
Creative Garments-Lower Parel	Italian
Ajanta Pharma Ltd.	Russian
Pcs Ltd.	Dutch
Iscc, Seepz	Chinese

Clients	Languge Course Offered
Dalal Consultancy Ltd.	Italian
Premier Auto	Italian
Afs,Seepz	Spanish
Shankar Jwellers,Seepz	Spanish
Hindustan Constructions	Chinese
L&T Infotech	Portuguese
E-Serve-Internat1onal	Spanish
Silicon Interfaces	Spanish
Dagapetro Chemicals	Mandarin
Jesons Corporation	Mandarin
Polaris Lab	Spanish
Marish Eleectronics	Japanese
Hcl - Baroda	Japanese
Anand Ritter Ltd.	German
Orient Syntex Ltd.	Italian
Jamuna Gases	Italian
Lemur Air Express	German
Capgemini Ltd.	Dutch
Iflex Solutions	Japanese
Datamatics	Chinese
Raymond	Chinese
Aditya Birla Group	Thai
Chandok Exports	Chinese

Clients	Languge Course Offered
Bharat Diamond Bourse	Chinese
Yamuna Gases Ltd	Italian Interpretation
Perfetti India Ltd	Italian Interpretation
Fiat India Ltd	Italian Training
Hotel J.w.marriot	Training
Hotel President	Italian Training
Hiranandani Construction	Italian Training
Morarji Brembana Ltd.	Italian Training
The Rennaisance	Training
The Leela	Interpretation

Students Speak

"Would like to thank Purohit Academy for the immense guidance and support in helping me clear IELTS. The comprehensive study materials helped me score high on the test and sail through without a hitch."

—Nilesh Bulsara

~~~

"I am now able to face my interviewers with confidence and poise. I am very positive of the outcome now."

—Alifiya M. Kutiyanaha:
(Personality Development Student)

~~~

"For me, the Academy has opened up a window of opportunity. The faculty is excellent and their expertise is immense. The difference between other Academies and Purohit's is that her each individual is involved. I am indebted to Mrs. Purohit for the amount of interest she's taken in helping me realise my dream."

—Gautam Shenoy *(GRE Student)*

~~~

"Anita mam taught us with full energy and enthusiasm."

—Pooja Ahuja *(GRE Student)*

~~~

"It was indeed a great learning experience and practice-oriented. Highly recommended."

—Deepanshu Bura *(Thai Student)*